Rosy's Little Book of Prose

Every day we weave our way and eventually we will find the place where we should be, whether it takes us back to old haunts or pastures new and as our paths entangle and some stop short when found their defined destiny with good time to spare whilst others can take all but a lifetime to find their resting peaceful place to end their final days ....

Rosy Mckenzie (October 2014)

Front cover photo: *Rosy's art, pastel on paper, sunset on beach.*

Dedication

"I dedicate this book to my mum and dad who showed me the way."

Photo of my dear mum and dad circa 1940s. 'Courting days.'

Acknowledgements

Thanks go to John Chenery for putting the book together, and for his help and inspiration overall.

Rosy's Little Book of Prose

Rosy Mckenzie

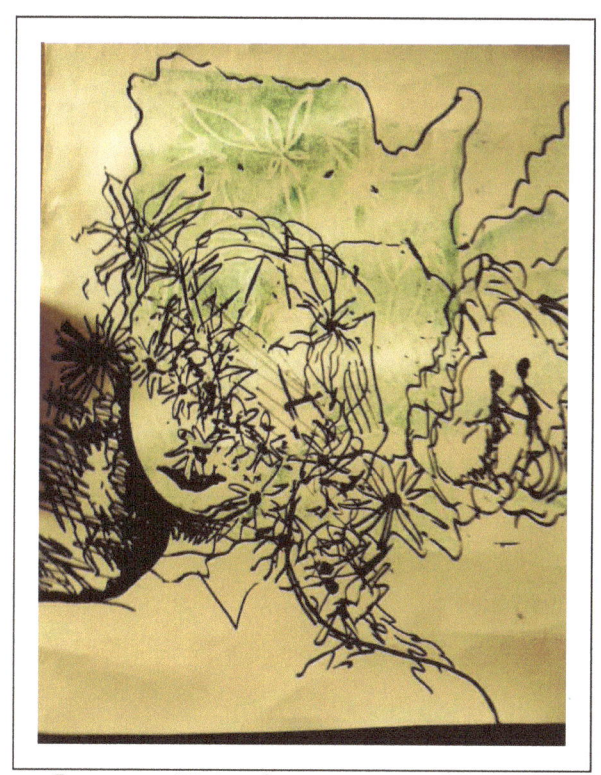

Rosy art: Vision loss conceptualisation

A Rosy Mckenzie publication 2019

Copyright

Text, artwork and photographs by Rosy Mckenzie.

Copyright © 2019 Rosy Mckenzie.
ISBN 978-0-244-18213-7

All rights reserved. This book or any portion thereof may not be reproduced or used in any manner whatsoever without the express written permission of the author except for the use of brief quotations in a book review or scholarly journal.

First published May 2019

A Rosy Mckenzie publication

WWW.RosyPoems.com

Formatted at *Fynevue* in England.

Index of Poems

Steel Magnolias 4

Remembering 6

Paths 8

Where is Home? 10

Moods 12

Seasons 14

My Three Amigos 16

Chinese Whispers 18

Metamorphosis 20

Months Ahead 23

Globalisation 26

Fat or Thin? 28

An Urban Fox 30

My Hat 32

Peace 33

A Fair Wind 36

Sniff 37

Cat in a Box: Not for Sox! 39

My Favourite Poems

Profile

I have enjoyed arts and crafts from a very young age. My mother remembers me doodling biro drawings of people at the beach or in town.

To this day I am creative albeit with certain challenges. As a naturally talented student of art I did an *Access to Art & Design* course at *South East Essex College* and attended *Central Saint Martin's* art college in London where I studied Ceramics, returning to *South East Essex College* to study Fine Art.

I had plans to train to be an art teacher and use my artistic talent as a pathway to a new career, but this was, unfortunately interrupted by a sudden loss of vision. This led me to be diagnosed with advanced glaucoma, a hereditary disease, which is degenerative and affects the optic nerve.

Rosy with her Guide Dog, Polly.

Up until 2010 my glaucoma was stable and managed with eye drops and I could see well with glasses or contact lenses. In later years my eyesight deteriorated and continues to do so.

I currently have a Guide Dog Polly, as although not completely blind am entitled to have one, to help me stay safe and mobile, as I am now registered severely sight impaired.

My art has changed gradually since losing my eyesight and where once I could give attention to fine detail in my work, I adapted to create more abstract work with sponges rather than brushes. Working in layers I can build up different colours to give a greater sense of depth to my work.

I have not only continued to pursue my artistic talent but have been lucky enough to attend The Royal College for the Blind in Hereford, through my local Job Centre and attained a qualification: NVQ Award in Business and Administration. I have also done volunteer work for the RNIB (Royal National Institute for the Blind) in London, worked for Family Lives as inbound call centre operative helping people with their emotional problems, as well as contract work with LOOK as a Project Assistant in a charity for blind and visually impaired children.

Since 2014 I have been writing poetry as an alternative creative outlet and I continue with some photography and have a Blog page on WordPress at RosyPoems.com with my poetry, art, photography, thoughts and favourite quotes.

Rosy Mckenzie (May 2019)

My Favourite Poems

Steel Magnolias

Rosy writes… *A woman who possess the strength of steel, yet the gentleness of a magnolia is a steel magnolia. USA Southern term - have you seen the film too? I was talking to a blind friend of mine in USA and she said I was a Steel Magnolia! I know lots of women who are too.*

Steel Magnolia is what I am, someone told me today
It was a blind friend I know from the USA

It means I have the will to carry on
and get through another day

With a gentle heart, and strength of steel
It is what I surely am and feel

Through all the adversity I have faced
For all the dreams that I have chased

Rosy's Little Book of Prose

The hills I have climbed, only to tumble down
And keep a smile, and try not to frown

As my dreams all turn to sand
And there is no one there to take my hand

I'll walk this life tall and alone
So please don't ask me on the phone

How are you today, cos fine I'll say!
What else is there to utter no burden I'll lay?

The strength of a Magnolia is Steel
So that is what I am and feel

Nothing will ever cast me down
I will get up again, and walk into town

And carry on in this hazy world
where now is dust when once was gold

I walk amid many women who like me
Steel Magnolias we will always be

To the very last we will not be cast down
We always smile there is no frown

Until the very final time
For when for us the sun no longer shines

Our hearts will linger on with love
And we will shine on you from above

My Favourite Poems

Remembering

Rosy art: Pastel on paper, sunset on beach.

Please say a prayer and have thoughts today
For all those near and far away…

Who have suffered under hands of atrocities
Whilst tempers outraged with terrible possibilities
In many parts of the World these mindless acts
To destroy our lives, we try and keep in tact
Pray for peace and kindness in this world
In Syria, Afghanistan and more
We don't hear all the news
Of places with no media views
Where innocent people suffer each day
In order that these madmen get their way
And destroy lives
It is barbaric
And such a waste of time ... precious time...
Please let these crazy minded people see the light
And of our planet observe the plight!
The icebergs are melting
The water is rising
The ozone layer is getter larger
Every day it will become harder
To maintain our World
As once we knew
As amid the chaos that does spew
How can this beautiful planet survive?
We know that good will always prevail
And will rise above evil
Amid the ashes of the world
I can see fresh new shoots rising
Because there will always be a way
To shine forth with courage
And save the day!

My Favourite Poems

Paths

Sometimes when I walk around Shrewsbury, I think for one moment I am still in Southend-on-Sea, or Hockley where I was born, maybe similar paths look the same...?

Different paths the same?

I walked along the road
It is a different path

But sometimes it feels just the same
As paths I've walked before

There are the trees
The cars
The houses
The people passing by

It could be any road
But one I've already walked…

Deja vu
Does it come to you?
As you walk along your path

The same things to do
The same things to say

But this path is different…
Come what may

Rosy art: mixed media on paper, Forest Colours

Rosy's Little Book of Prose

Rosy photo: A well-trodden path (2019)

The bird flew over, many miles away
And there I saw it again, on my fence today!

No matter where I be, whether in country, or in town,
In my casual clothes, or even a posh gown

Different roads, and different folks,
But it all just feels the same

Nothing is really different,
In this lifelong game.

My Favourite Poems

Where is Home?

Where is home? Yes, where is home? Home is where the heart is...

Rosy photo: Southend-on-Sea, Essex, sunset 2018.

Rosy's Little Book of Prose

Spring is in the air
Yellow surge of daffodil…

A bird is singing
High up on the hill

There is a touch of hope
Deep within our hearts
As spring begins to start

Excitement with some sunshine
And green grass growing strong
In nature new life is budding

Though it's slow
That newness is aglow
With frosty mornings
Still all alive with twinkle
Like a magical garden bright
Let's walk by The Dingle!

Shrewsbury is very nice
Lots of greenery to be seen
This is my new abode
I was very keen...

Rosy art: Acrylic on board, Yellow flowers (2017)

But I miss the sea gently lapping on the coast edge and shore
I long to feel the sand between my toes once more….

The seaside has always been my home - Southend-on-Sea
So where is just the right place, for little old me!

Moods

A little reminder - Sometimes people when they are having a bad day or upset themselves will take it out on you but never take this personally it is all about them and how they are feeling, our actions and words reflect our inner being. It's all about me!

People may shout
And put you down
But don't frown
Be brave and put on a smile
Cos in a while they will see
How horrid and silly they can be
Just stay calm
Avoid the harm
It's their mindset not yours inside
Though it hurts
Those nasty words
There's a tear in your eye
As you try not to cry
But their premise it surely is
So, don't get in a tizz
When people can't cope
It's easier you see
To blame little ole 'me'
Than to face the truth
Of what they themselves behold
And are being so cold
To you

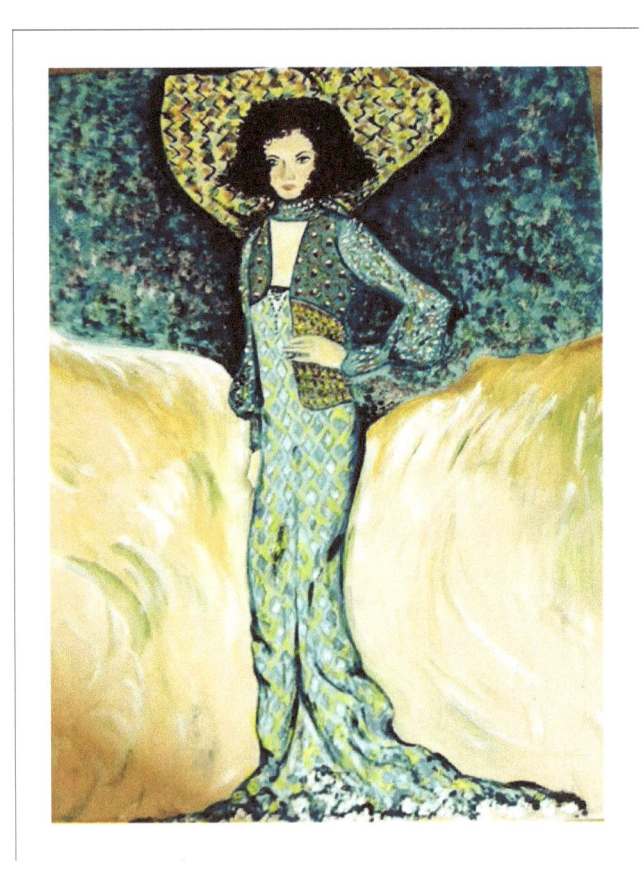

Rosy art: Acrylic on canvas board, Klimt style (2011)

Rosy's Little Book of Prose

Every action you take
And every word you utter
Is all about you
You see

So, think carefully
What you say and do
The little saying is so true
Treat others as you…

Would be treated yourself
And put all that bad feeling on the shelf
Follow your heart
Right from the start

Don't let their noise
Drown out your voice
Karma comes in the end

To set the balance straight
As you walk through that gate
To peace and happiness

Rosy photo: Lily of the Valley flowers (2018)

Peace Love Hope Respect Karma

Seasons

Seasons, a poem by me, with a visually impaired view

What a thing the spring
The pretty daffodils ... where?
If only for a few days and hours
The lovely smell...
That newness
The dew, the damp, cool rain...
To whirl and bring warmth again
I feel it not see it
It's ok I love it
I know, it's spring...

Now it's summer
There's a bummer!
It's too hot is it not
No air conditioning here
Oh dear!
The warmth through my feet
Wearing sandals what a treat!
Walking in the sea
As the tide comes in
Now there's a thing
I feel it not see it
It's OK I love it
I know, it's summer…

Rosy art: Springtime tree, acrylic on canvas.

Rosy's Little Book of Prose

So, autumn…
Here you are
The door is ajar
The leaves are rustling
Everyone is hustling!
Getting ready for Christmas!
No! It's too early
But the leaves are all twirly
Colourful, aren't they?
I feel it not see it
It's OK I love it
I know it's Autumn…

Winter oh brrr, it's cold!
It's grey out there
So, I'm told...
It's all festive with Christmas joy
I love that feeling ... oh boy!
Snow crunch on ground
OK it's found
The white stuff under my toes
With cold it glows
I feel it not see it
It's OK I love it
I know, it's winter…

Rosy art: Autumn, acrylic on canvas.

I can feel it, hear it, touch it, sense it... it's here...it's ok... isn't it... what's that saying...
You don't need sight to have vision...
But isn't that a division though … between light and dark
What a lark!
I'm ok ...

My Three Amigos

This is a poem about my three children, Chrissy, Nick and Rob

They talked to me
These three little chaps
They would laugh
And chatter
About this and that
Conversations
Silly and fun
Their little lives
Had just begun
Those days
They seem to last forever
And I would never, never
At that time
Believe it true
How grown up
They would become
Phew!
But time passes
Quickly it does
Lots of fun tears and fuss
Ado about serious things
And laughter
We all just want
And need
A happy ever after
A struggle it has been
With adversity

My Favourite Poems

Rosy's Little Book of Prose

All unseen
But today
I'm feeling proud
And I would really like
To say aloud
To my three amigos
My children as such
How I love you so very much
Each day I dearly think of you
And when I am feeling blue
I remember all our happy days
Which now seem so far away
When you were small
And life was cheerful
If only a little tearful then
Now you're doing good
In the World so wide
Busy bees now
Grown
Not at my side
But in my heart
Forever it's true
I love you dearly, through and through…

So, take the time to just say hi, as you and your busy day goes by
When you're young, important tasks, are only but a trivial mask!
Cos what's important is to spend time with those you love
As soon they're gone to heaven above
And in your heart, they will surely stay
Until we meet again one day
As Grandad often said to me,
whilst we were having
cups of tea!

My Favourite Poems

Chinese Whispers

Rosy writes…

A little birdy told me so
Did you know?
This has happened just today!
Oh, I say!
Really!

Well, I'd never have thought it true
And what just happened to you know who!
I'll let you know
I'll tell you why
Cos that birdy again might just drop by!

And tell me more news
You never know
It could be so
It's true!
Through and through

Not a word of gossip for my ears
Just the words and wonder with a few tears

Don't you hear things that people say
But do Chinese whispers get in the way!

Be careful to your friends what you utter
For some, telling tales is like bread and butter!

Words get misconstrued
And misused

Our lives can be made to look so bad
By someone who is quite simply mad

Or mean
With a mind unclean

So, don't listen to what people say
Until the evidence is here to stay

People love to chit and chat about this and that
And that is that

Rosy art: Sunset Inspired - three canvas acrylic on board (2016)

Metamorphosis

Rosy writes…
Metamorphosis even the ugliest of bugs can change into something beautiful!

An ugly bug sat on a stem
With stripes of green I looked again
Red yellow orange and black
Certainly, there was no lack

Was it, horrid no, no, no!
But it was a creepy crawly, I think so!
With a vivid skin all of a shine
It really was just fine...

A caterpillar it was I shout!
With black curly legs all hairy about!
It ate and ate with all its might
The lettuces green stuff what a plight!

The garden veg was all askew
As it munched its way through and through
Then when it had had more than enough
It changed so quick it must have been tough!

Into a chrysalis all white and still
It hung on the branch it had had its fill
For a time, it seemed to ponder there
It did not move nor have a care

Rosy's Little Book of Prose

Then one day it burst through the shell
Oh my! And now I could tell
A beautiful butterfly so delicate it was now
So, what a wondrous thing I could not see how

That ugly bug could turn for real
Into something so beautiful, it was surreal!

So, when you are walking down the street
And an ugly bug you chance to meet
Just remember the possible fact
That their ugliness may not stay in tact

A spark of magic could touch their soul
And from a very ugly ghoul
They could change into a being with beauty and love
All blessed from somewhere in the heavens above

And light the way to being good
From hence once a horridness they stood
There is always a chance for bugs to change
And for their nastiness to then be strange!

And so being good all through and through
And stop making others feel so blue
A butterfly is a thing of beauty
And it shows to us to our very duty

To be kind and caring all the time
And that from an ugly bug you can turn to be loving and kind
So that's the end of my tale
I hope it is to some avail

My Favourite Poems

**That I say to you there is room for change each day
To lead a better caring life, I say!**

**So that's all I have to utter for this time
I hope you enjoy this metamorphosis of a rhyme!**

Rosy art: Butterfly acrylic on board (2017)

Rosy's Little Book of Prose

Months Ahead

Rosy writes…
Months Ahead - the whole year and here we go again!

January you are dark and cold
It is dreary no pretty lights to behold
Christmas is over the cheer is done
And now its wintery and not much fun

February the wind is blowing a gust
Nights are drawing, out only just
It is very frosty still underfoot too
Forsythia shows a small bud for you

March winds, March hares!
Look forward to Spring if you dare
Is there a crocus peeping through the snow?
That colourful bud, you never know!

April come she will (a chorus)
And with it, spring blooms do fill
Our gardens full of song
(Simon and Garfunkel to whom that song does belong!)

May well ok… a bit warmer now to be sure
I can leave open my door
The sun is shining, the lambs are growing
The grass is need, for sure, of mowing!

My Favourite Poems

June, it's all in full bloom
Holidays and sunny days
Gentle rain just warm and hazy
Oh, how this heat just makes me feel lazy

July the days are long though they are falling shorter now
Children on holiday from school, what fun! Wow!
Swimming in the pool or sea
Sunny garden and afternoon tea

August die she must… but not yet
(The duo did some good tunes, you bet!)
The sun is shining the days last for ever
No, it can't be September soon back to school no, not never!

September the summer is now a memory gone by
Back to school and alarm clocks my oh my!
Routines and homework once more here we go
Soon be Halloween, Bonfire night, and Christmas in tow!

October, well it's in the middle
Between the summer and winter, for a diddle!
Nothing happens but the leaves start to fall
And there is a fox out there starting to call

November, November it's here November, November
And we all remember… don't we?
Bonfire night and fireworks plenty more
Whilst all the pets hide behind the cupboard door

Rosy's Little Book of Prose

December at last is fun loving and exciting
Christmas carols and snow ball fighting (if we get snow of course!)
Presents under the tree and lovely dinner
I think this month is really the winner!

What do you think?
What is your favourite month of the year and why?

Rosy art: 2015

Globalisation

Globalisation, me dear!
The World is a much smaller place these days, can we share it fairly and in peace...

I think the time has come near
When we must hold dear

This much we must dare
And be bold and to share

Every creed colour religion and nation
Without any frustration

Goodwill and love
Does shines down from above

But our planet is heaving
And no one is leaving

There is no escape
We have made many a mistake

In our evolution
Without thought or solution

The planet needs saving
Whilst new iPhones we are craving

The water is rising
The sun hotly shining

As icebergs melt
Depleting ozone is felt

People rush round
Much importance is found

In activity trivial
Nonsensical ritual

Wars never ending
With no peace transcending

Nuclear war could transpire
That would destroy every desire

In one moment, we'd be gone
There would be no song

So, wouldn't it be better for us
To not make so much fuss

And our differences put aside
So, no one need hide

Globalisation must bring us together
Because none of us are really that clever

So, do you have an idea?
To work this all out me dear!

Fat or Thin?

Rosy writes... *Imbalance in the western world; people are paying to join dieting clubs to lose weight whilst in the other parts of the world people are starving.*

Where do I begin? In the western world we eat too much

Grub it is abundant
How often do we hear, "I'm on a diet!"
And then it's all redundant

You find the tin
With the cookies in
And before you know it
You have blown it!

Whilst in Africa
The menu is dust
A child walks six miles for water
And a tiny crust

Thankful for a small meal
This is the deal
Dirty water only to drink
Does this make you think?

The imbalance of the world it's very true
Is apparent both to me and you
So, whilst you eat your big dinner
Others just grow thinner and thinner

Rosy's Little Book of Prose

Isn't it about time it was fair?
And all of us who really care
Could see clear to assist the plight
Of those who hunger, out of sight

Helpless we may feel today
But surely there is some way
That life could be fair
And if we really care

Make the world a better place
On every table with food grace

Rosy photo: Meals 2019

My Favourite Poems

An Urban Fox

Rosy writes… *when I lived in Southend-on-Sea, it was common to see a fox walking down my street, they had become very urbanised being ousted out of their natural habitat by man and foraging in bins for food...*

**A fox walked by my house today
He was mangy and so sad
The countryside for which he yearned
Was no more to be had**

**His tail was bent, his fur was ruffled
His voice it was even muffled**

**This urban place had called him in
Amidst all the traffic and the din**

**What a shame our wildlife has to seek
And makes this fox so very weak**

**Foraging bins and rubbish to chew
Scraps so very far and few**

**Will make him wobble…
And unsteady on his feet, old burgers he will gobble**

**Stale chips a plenty too
Not much of a treat**

Rosy's Little Book of Prose

It is so very, very sad
Has this world gone mad?

By the railway he finds his home
And looks so very sad and alone

Not a beautiful fox as he should be
With sleek fur and lovely face for all to see

Our countryside is going to waste
As more houses built with haste

So, foxes...
In little boxes...

I think not
They should not be forgot...

Take them back to the woods I say!
And let them enjoy their natural way!

In the forests and the fields right now
I really wonder how

This world is changing not all for the best
As we put our wildlife to the test

So, what ideas have you today?
To make this fox happy and find his natural way?

My Favourite Poems

My Hat

Rosy writes... *My Hat and that is that! I bought a hat to keep out the glare as when you have glaucoma bright light is not good!*

**I bought this hat
Not to share
It's very good
Keeps out the glare
For my eyes
They are so glaucomatised**

**I do so try
Not to cry**

**But the mist is creeping
Inside I'm weeping**

**But each day
I must find a way**

**To find some joy
And oh boy!**

Rosy photo: My Hat

**Easy it is not
I've not forgot**

**The wonders I can see
Being taken from me**

**I'll try to adjust
It is a must.**

**So, sounds I hear,
Become now dear.**

**So, sing me a song
It won't take long.**

**To brighten my day
In a different way!**

Rosy's Little Book of Prose

Peace

Rosy writes… *I chat on an app on my phone called Vorail with people all over the World, they are mostly blind or visually impaired, like myself.*

Happy New Year Ditty
If a bit daft, but could be witty

I was walking along the road one day
When an American passed by my way

I said howdy as you do
Cos he could be a Cowboy you never knew!

Then a Spanish lady drinking her tea
Sat right next to me

Como estas?! I said out loud
And did a flamenco dance…
of which I'm proud!

In Cuba I took a stance
A big cigar I took a chance

It looked so good but made me cough
And everyone around me began to laugh

Rosy art: Poppy watercolour.

My Favourite Poems

So, I sailed away to where Eskimos abide
A chilly igloo, I looked inside!

They offered me fish and snug clothes
I then felt warm right to my toes

Hotter climes I did then seek
I then just took a peek

A Native American in his teepee tall
With amazing headdress, and wondrous squaw

Then to Africa I took a chance
Happy faces and a war dance!

Then to Australia, cos I stood on my head!
A kangaroo bounced right by my bed!

In India, wow! It's Bollywood
I never dreamed they really could

Dance so brightly, saris so pretty
To an amazing Indian ditty

So, to these places and many more
I peeped inside through an open door

The World is full of beautiful beings
It's not all bad it's for the seeing

Happy folks just making their way
Is what we all do from day to day

So, strive for peace and understanding
Please don't be so cross and demanding!

Love your neighbour it is true
Is what I say to you

Peace Love Joy Serenity   Hope

It is something with
…which we need to cope

Our World it is an amazing place
So please do have the grace

To treat it and others kindly now
So that we may see how

To save it from the perils of life
No more guns, greed, wars,
… violence, pollution, strife

And keep it as it truly began
A beautiful place for beast and man

Wildlife simplicity peace and wonder
On this note I leave you to ponder

Rosy art: Sunflower watercolour.

A Fair Wind

Rosy writes… *time moves on we have sorrows and happiness and life is ever changing.*

**A Fair Wind blew it bought a change
The sun shone brightly through the haze
The world still spun
And life moves on
We cannot stop it
Our feet are walking
We are talking
And there is peace
Let sorrows die
And the past filter behind us
Bring joy and happiness
On this new moon
As we find a new way
This day is for change
And happiness, and hope
Our days move fast
We must enjoy them
And cherish our dreams
Life ever changing
The ups, the downs
Bring the good things to us
And enjoy the days we have before us
Keep the sorrows tucked away
And keep a smile, and enjoy your life
Be grateful while your heart beats**

Rosy photo: Local church

Sniff

Sniff is something that I do…
The smells are great, but not for you!

Humans like to sniff flowers
Coffee, perfume, aftershave
To those things… I simply wave!

Cos I'm a dog with no monologue
I sniff the ground, there's lots to do
The grass, the squirrels
And other dogs' pooh!

Some dogs they work with their noses
And no one quite supposes
Or even comprehends this much.

I can smell it from afar without a touch

The drugs hidden away; the airport rogues, that think smuggling drugs is in the vogue.
Us clever doggies catch them quick, before we even have a lick!

Our sense of smell is so fantastic, it stretches far even better than elastic!
It drives us crazy these lovely whiffs, and nothing is there better than to sniff!

So have respect for our clever noses, cos no-one really supposes
We are that smart or can do that much at all, but we sniff a lot and will recall

Anything that needs to be found, in the airport or on the ground
And when we go to the park, it's better to sniff than to bark!

My Favourite Poems

Rosy photos: Polly Guide Dog

**I drive my owner crazy I have to say too,
As she waits while I sniff and nearly turns blue!**

**Cos, I sniff, and I sniff, and sniff even more
Right up to the moment we reach our front door!**

Rosy's Little Book of Prose

Cat in a Box: Not for Sox!

Rosy writes… *I got a new Christmas Tree it arrived in a box....my cat Katy loves sitting in boxes especially if they come from Amazon!*

A lovely box
Too big for sox!
But it's just right
I won't put up a fight
As I sit here
In this box
Not meant for sox!

A Christmas tree
Inside was found
Ready for the season
And that is why
I sit in this box
Not meant for sox!

For no particular reason!
Sox need only
A box much smaller
Cos a Christmas Tree is taller
So, more room in my box
Not meant for sox!

To jump around
And be a pussycat clown
Don't get me wrong
Small boxes are cool

Rosy photo: Katy cat in a box!

My Favourite Poems

But you'd be a fool
If you didn't think
This box was fun
Just as the Christmas season
Has begun
Cats love boxes
For Christmas trees or soxes!

So, I'll sit here
Without a fear
And peep out
Or hide
And disappear
Meow!

Merry Christmas cheer
Will soon be here!

Rosy art: Christmas tree

Other Photo Credits

Steel Magnolias © J. Chenery 2006
My Three Amigos © Rosy Mckenzie
Urban Fox © J. Chenery 2017

Lightning Source UK Ltd.
Milton Keynes UK
UKHW021133030821
388210UK00002B/40